Bruno Santi

LEONARDO
DA VINCI

SCALA

CONTENTS

© Copyright 1990 by SCALA Group S.p.A.,
Antella (Florence)
Design: Daniele Casalino
Photographs: SCALA (M. Falsini, M. Sarri) except nos.
18 and 30 (British Museum); 42, 43, 69 (National
Gallery, London); 66 (National Gallery, Washington);
the drawings from the Royal Library, Windsor, are
reproduced by Fac-simile
Printed in Italy by: Amilcare Pizzi S.p.A.- arti grafiche
Cinisello Balsamo (Milan), 2005

1. Leonardo's house at Vinci

His life

Leonardo was born in the village of Vinci, between the Tuscan cities of Empoli and Pistoia, on 15 April 1452. His father, Ser Piero d'Antonio was a notary. The future artist's mother was a woman from Anchiano named Caterina, who later married a peasant. Despite his illegitimacy, Leonardo was treated with affection in his father's house, where he was reared and educated. In 1468 his grandfather Antonio died, and the following year the paternal family moved to Florence. The boy's precocious artistic gifts led his father to send him to study with the most versatile and sought-after Florentine master of the time: the sculptor, painter, and goldsmith Andrea Verrocchio. Little is known about Leonardo's work under this master, and there are few examples of Verrocchio's painting. According to tradition (a tradition confirmed by scholarly analysis), Leonardo was responsible for the angel and the landscape in the *Baptism of Christ*, a panel now in the Uffizi, which certainly came from Verrocchio's shop. This is where Leonardo's artistic personality began to develop. From 1472 on, he was enrolled as a master in the Company of Painters, so we can assume his apprenticeship to Verrocchio had ended by that

year, though he remained in the master's shop. Leonardo was attracted to every sort of artistic discipline, driven by an unparalleled curiosity and by his ability to complement those disciplines with his scientific knowledge, the fruit of tireless investigation into natural phenomena, which he observed acutely.

In 1480 he was a member of that extraordinary academy, the garden of San Marco, under the patronage of Lorenzo the Magnificent. This was Leonardo's first venture into sculpture, an art which naturally attracted him because of the completeness of its very nature. In that same year he was commissioned to paint the *Adoration of the Magi* for the church of San Donato Scopeto, just outside Florence (the work is now in the Uffizi). But the Florentine environment had become too narrow and frustrating for him. Perhaps the fact that he was not one of the four masters invited to paint the walls of the Sistine Chapel drove him to seek a change of scene, or perhaps it was his natural restlessness which made him constantly try out new experiences, looking for new creative horizons.

In 1482, in any case, he presented himself to the

Duke of Milan, Lodovico Sforza, "Il Moro", with a letter in which he lists and describes his own capacities, including his talents as a civil engineer and designer of war machinery. His welcome in the Lombard city was favorable. He lodged with the De Predis brothers, painters, in the Porta Ticinese quarter, and in 1483 he was already engaged in decorating the great ancona (altarpiece) in the chapel of the Immacolata in the church of San Francesco Grande. Thus he painted the *Virgin of the Rocks* in the two versions now in Paris and London. During these years he was also occupied with the most vexatious and thankless assignment of his career: the equestrian monument to Francesco Sforza, for which he made countless sketches, drawings, models, constantly testing new ideas and techniques of casting. In 1489-90 he prepared the decoration of the Castello of the Sforzas for the approaching wedding of Gian Galeazzo Sforza and Isabella of Aragon. His activity gradually extended to one new area after another. In 1494 hydraulics became his concern, and he devoted himself to the reclamation of the Sforza lands in the Lombard plain. In 1495, however, the fresco of the *Last Supper* in Santa Maria delle Grazie became the almost exclusive object of his studies. The work was to be finished only in 1498. A year later Louis XII, king of France, invaded the Duchy of Milan. Leonardo abandoned the city and went to Mantua and Venice. In 1503 he was back in Florence, where he

was commissioned to fresco the great Council Chamber in the Palazzo della Signoria, along with Michelangelo. Leonardo was assigned, as his subject, the *Battle of Anghiari*, while Michelangelo was to do the *Battle of Càscina*. Once again, Leonardo's eagerness to find new techniques for the execution of the painting prevented him from finishing the work. Probably in this same year he painted *La Gioconda* (Mona Lisa), which also remained unfinished.

Between June 1506 and September 1507 Leonardo returned once again to Milan. There, in 1512, the new Duke, Massimiliano Sforza, was installed. On 24 September of that year, Leonardo set out for Rome with his disciples; there he conducted mathematical and scientific studies of every kind. From there he traveled to several other cities, though always returning to Rome.

In May 1513 he accepted the invitation of the French king Francis I, who called him to Amboise. There Leonardo remained until his death. During his French years the artist created plans for festivities, but also continued with his hydrological projects, intended for several French rivers. On 23 April 1519 he made his will, remembering in it all those who were close to him. On 2 May of the same year he died, and was buried in the church of Saint Florentin at Amboise. During the religious wars of the sixteenth century his grave was violated and his remains scattered.

Verrocchio and Leonardo

Andrea del Verrocchio (born in 1435) had a renowned workshop in Florence, producing works in every artistic field: marble and bronze sculpture, painting, and examples of the goldsmith's art. Verrocchio's personality concludes the most active period of the Florentine Renaissance: far, by now, from the heroic manner of Masaccio and Donatello, he — and with him, other contemporary artists like the Pollaiolo brothers — concerned himself with a more naturalistic representation of the human form. Verrocchio's sculpture is well-known (the bronze *David* in the Bargello, the *Doubting Thomas* group on the facade of Orsanmichele, and the Colleoni monument in Venice are his most familiar works); but there is much uncertainty about his activity as a painter. The only panel surely conceived and executed in his shop is the *Baptism of Christ* in the

Uffizi, which seems, when analyzed critically, an anthology of pictorial styles. The Christ and the Baptist possess the typical Florentine firm draftsmanship. The line, rich in movement, immediately suggests the master's sculptures. As we shall see, the angel on the left and the landscape, executed by Leonardo, are totally different. Andrea's shop, for that matter, welcomed several artists (including Botticelli and Perugino) who, having completed their training elsewhere, felt a need to confront their art with his. The shop's undeniable prestige and its reputation for attracting many patrons no doubt influenced Ser Piero's decision to send his son there to learn the art of painting. There Leonardo's meditations were to find the instruments most suitable to their figurative depiction. In fact, his first experience was gained in the space assigned him in the *Bap-*

2. Andrea del Verrocchio and Leonardo
Baptism of Christ
180 x 152 cm
Florence, Uffizi

4

5

3, 4. Andrea del Verrocchio and Leonardo
Baptism of Christ, details
Florence, Uffizi

5. Drawing of a landscape
Florence, Uffizi Prints and Drawings Rooms

tism. Andrea del Verrocchio died in Venice in 1488.

In his very first experience as a painter, the above-mentioned angel and the landscape background in Verrocchio's panel of the *Baptism of Christ*, Leonardo already reveals his technical maturity, his mastery of the means of expression (drawing and color, in this case), as well as his formal maturity. We can see how these two details are notably different from the rest of the painting. The stiff, almost metallic-looking palm on the left, the figure of Christ and the vigorous Baptist, have nothing in common with the adolescent angel whose outline is caressed and moulded by the light reflected also in the long waving hair. And they have nothing in common with the vast landscape which opens out just above the angels' heads. This view of nature is much more complex than the schematic landscapes to which fifteenth-century Florentine painting was accustomed: a winding river in a valley dotted with stylized cypresses and poplars. There, every form served to measure the space that was to be inhabited by man; here, there is no boundary, and you sense a broad nature waiting to be explored and discovered. We must therefore underline the total novelty of Leonardo's painting compared with his master's style or that of anyone else who may have had a hand in this painting. But this novelty is an achievement which owes its development to what the young artist found in Verrocchio's shop, although the pictorial conclusions — as can be seen — are completely personal and original: an advanced knowledge in the field of human anatomy, an absolute mastery of the depiction of movement, a great ability in modeling the material to the point of creating effects of vibrant chiaroscuro and a careful study of the portrayal of emotions. It is also true that all these elements bring us back more to Verrocchio's sculpture than to his painting, of which, in any case, we have very few examples. Still, these were no doubt the goals of Leonardo's studies with Verrocchio. During those years the younger man enriched his natural artistic bent with tecnical skills, receiving the means to reach at least a first stage in his artistic expression, which already appears quite distinct and more complex. In it, nothing of the master's style survives, but the development of Leonardo's art would be inconceivable without this patrimony of elements offered by Verrocchio's shop, with its wide range of activities. The relationship between master and pupil must be seen then in this perspective.

Florentine painting around 1480

For Florence, the years around 1480 were a time of relative political stability. When the final outbursts of hostility to the Medici were suppressed harshly in 1478, at the time of the Pazzi conspiracy, the personal regime of Lorenzo di Piero de' Medici was confirmed by popular support. There was also a total absence of political personalities who could arrest the slow but inevitable change from a republican form of government to a virtual dictatorship, though the magistrature and the traditional institutions were formally respected. Moreover, Lorenzo de' Medici was to become the "needle of the scale", in Machiavelli's expression, of the politics of all Italy, preserving the equilibrium among the powers that dominated the peninsula (Milan, Venice, the Papal States, Naples). Once the equilibrium was destroyed, then Italy was to fall immediately into the hands of foreign monarchies such as France and Spain which, having unified their own national territories under the crown, could think of expanding their power beyond their natural boundaries.

This period also saw an intense production in the city. True, Florence was no longer the only Italian city that could express the most progressive and, qualitatively, the highest art. Centers like Urbino and Mantua were developing, while Venice, with the Bellinis, was entering its finest period, the Cinquecento, and Rome, with the patron-Popes at the end of the century was to initiate those artistic enterprises that would make the city the absolute capital of Italian art in the following century. Florence, nevertheless, was still the place where artistic debate was at its liveliest. In 1466, the last survivor of the Renaissance's first artistic generation, Donatello, had died, and three years later, in 1469, the most interesting painter of the second generation, Fra Filippo Lippi, who had initiated a more illustrative and ornate form of painting, followed him to the grave. The active painters in the city then were Alessio Baldovinetti (1425-1499), Andrea del Verrocchio (1435-1488), Antonio (ca. 1432-1498) and Piero (1441-1496) del Pollaiolo, Domenico del

6

7

7. Alessio Baldovinetti, Annunciation
Florence, Uffizi

6. Antonio del Pollaiolo
Hercules and Antaeus
Florence, Uffizi

8. Domenico Ghirlandaio, Visitation
Florence, Santa Maria Novella

8

9

8 Ghirlandaio (1449-1494), to name only the most important.

Baldovinetti had made a timid attempt to introduce into Florence the rigorous manner of Piero della Francesca, though he retained only Piero's firm geometrical structure in the construction of human forms. Otherwise, Baldovinetti was a rather delicate painter, close to Fra Filippo Lippi in his taste for color and his felicitous decorative motives. The Pollaiolo brothers brought to Florentine painting new energy and power which they expressed in alert, athletic figures (such as the *Hercules and Antaeus* in the Uffizi and the *Dancing Youths* in the Villa La Gallina, near Florence). But even when they painted religious subjects (the *Altarpiece with three Saints* in San Miniato al Monte), they were able to give the subject a general impression of vitality. These same characteristics are found in their sculpture and their rare examples of goldsmith work (like the panel with the *Nativity* of the silver altar of San Giovanni Battista) which have remained to demonstrate their versatility as artists.

Domenico del Ghirlandaio was quite another personality. A gifted illustrator and narrator, and a skilled portrait-painter, he was also influenced by the naturalistic vein of the Flemish artists, represented in Florence by the *Adoration of the Shepherds* (also known as the *Portinari Triptych*, now in the Uffizi), by Hugo van der Goes; the painting probably arrived in Florence in 1478. In his fresco cycles (*Life of the Virgin and the Baptist* in Santa Maria Novella, *Stories of Saint Francis* in Santa Trinita), Ghirlandaio masterfully introduced the life of the leading Florentine families of the time and portrayed for us the environment of the city. In his altarpieces, especially the *Nativity* in Santa Trinita, the Flemish influence is more evident in the limpid light of the background, the crystalline landscapes, and in the realistic depiction of the shepherds.

With these older masters, younger artists of the rising generation were asserting themselves: Alessandro Filipepi, known as Botticelli (born in 1455), 9 Filippino Lippi (born in 1457), both active in the Pollaiolo brothers' shop, each of whom would later develop a highly personal style, rich in formal beauty, with a strain of melancholy in Botticelli's case and a gift for fantastic and complex invention in the case of Filippino. And finally, Leonardo himself.

This was the varied environment, with its articulated personalities and artistic expressions, that Leonardo found in Florence when he began his training as an artist in the school of Andrea del Verrocchio.

9. Sandro Botticelli
Annunciation
Florence, San Martino alla Scala

The Annunciation in the Uffizi

This painting has been in the Uffizi since 1867. It came from the church of San Bartolomeo a Monteoliveto, in the environs of Florence. Traditional criticism has assigned this panel to the young Leonardo da Vinci, still working, though with independence and confident mastery, in the shop of Verrocchio. No historian or biographer, including Vasari, mentions this work, but we should note that the attribution stems from a simple consideration of the quality of the painting, which could not be by Verrocchio or by any other pupil of his. In particular the broad landscape in the background, despite intruding elements which suggest human presence (the ships and the river harbor), so unusual in Leonardo, brings us back to Leonardo's meditations on nature, with the white peaks of very high mountains which stand out against the pale blue of the sky. Similarly, the beauty of the faces, from the very young and dazed Madonna to the noble profile of the angel, is convincingly Leonardo's. The composition is extremely simple: a group of dark trees, a carpet of grass and flowers with vibrant leaves, a stone parapet behind the Virgin, the outer walls and the entrance of a country villa. Verrocchio's style is perceptible in secondary details, though they are handled with a fullness Andrea never achieved in painting: the rich drapery, the lectern with marble reliefs of extraordinary refinement, derived from the bronze tomb of Giovanni and Piero de' Medici in San Lorenzo. Leonardo seems to be using his master's repertory in order to free himself gradually of it, moving towards works where his own genius can finally express itself with all the ideas and formal achievements of which he is capable. The general impression of this work, which still follows the traditional iconography of fifteenth-century Annunciations, is of an intensity found in no other Florentine painting of this period. Obviously, then, in making an attribution, scholars have insisted on the young Leonardo.

10. Annunciation
98 x 217 cm
Florence, Uffizi

11-12. Annunciation, details
Florence, Uffizi

11

13

14

13. *Annunciation, detail of the landscape*
Florence, Uffizi

14. *Drawing of a woman's head*
Florence, Uffizi Prints and Drawings
Rooms

15. *Annunciation*
14 x 59 cm
Paris, Louvre

16, 17. *Annunciation, details*
Paris, Louvre

The Annunciation in the Louvre

This was the central panel of a predella, which recent scholarship has linked with the altarpiece known as the *Madonna di Piazza* in the cathedral of Pistoia, painted by Lorenzo di Credi, a fellow-pupil with Leonardo in Verrocchio's shop (ca. 1478-1485). Critics have unanimously attributed this panel to Leonardo. Even within its limited dimensions, the painting's structure is complex. Note, for example, the spatial articulations represented by the stone parapet placed at a right angle, echoed in the wooden benches set beside and behind the Virgin. In this setting, indirectly constructed, the figures of the angel and the Virgin are introduced with great authority. The Virgin here is individualized with greater coherence than her counterpart in the Uffizi, and is enhanced by exquisite color contrast, such as that between the very dark blue of her dress and the pale blue of her cloak. The angel also indicates precious study of material and color: the forearm covered with ochre velvet, the delicately draped vermilion cloak. But the landscape is particularly original: the garden with its little low trees, so remote from all conventional depiction, and the background where, in the light blue sky, only faintly darker, subtle peaks of high mountains can be discerned.

16

17

18

Action and movement

21 The *Adoration* of Leonardo is an undoubtedly impressive painting also because the scene is unusually crowded and is made even more fantastic by the contrast between the figures in the light and the groups immersed in almost total darkness. The painting has as well the disturbing fascination of an unfinished masterpiece. Leonardo started painting it only after a tormented period of preparation, whose stages can be reconstructed through the surviving drawings. On the one hand, it is interesting to see how his initial idea of an *Adoration of the Shepherds*, drawn from the most commonplace traditional iconography, was soon rejected and extended to involve a whole throng of humanity in the sacred event. But at the same time, we cannot consider the Uffizi panel as a simple sum of sketches added one to the other. It is, instead, the fruit of the twenty-nine-year old artist's attention to the world around him and the formal concepts that study had

inspired. In fact, Leonardo had devoted himself to the investigation of human physiognomy: from the wrinkled faces of old people to the smooth profiles of adolescents. His observations of the real consistency of the human body and anatomy led him to draw the abandoned corpse of Piero Baroncelli, 19 hanged in 1478 because of his connection with the Pazzi conspiracy against the Medici. Leonardo analyzed emotions and attitudes, in faces, in limbs, in the figures' poses, in the fall of drapery. And he also studied the movements and expressive capacities of 20 animals. In plants, too, he was prompt to seize on every sense of life, every form. Finally, he carried out authentic scientific observations, stemming from his interest in humanity and in everything man tirelessly creates. But in this work the depiction of movement is supremely important; it is in fact one of the figurative components of Leonardo's apprenticeship with Verrocchio and is a part of the expres-

sive tendency of this phase of fifteenth-century Florentine painting. A basic artistic problem in the early Renaissance was the proper insertion of the human figure in space. When this problem had been solved and overcome, the new motive of artistic content — movement — was to concern a generation of painters, beginning with Andrea del Castagno, around the middle of the century. But while it represented for them only a further development in art's expressive capacities, for Leonardo it was an essential element in his own system, which made philosophical and pictorial speculation coincide. Movement is the foundation of life, and more, it is also an instrument for the expression of emotions. The figure "will not in itself be praiseworthy if it does not express, as fully as possibile, the passion of its spirit with action". If this is the fundamental tenet of Leonardo's artistic expression (and the panel of the *Adoration* is its first true realization), then the consequences in the figurative field must be a profound investigation of the concept of movement, until *every* elementary particle of painting is directed towards achieving that *sfumato*, the subtlety, which "modeling the figures without lines, but only with lights and shadows, aims at making tangible the continuity of the world of appearances with the hidden world of forces", (Marinoni).

These, then, are the compositional elements of this extraordinary work, which appears, in its unfinished state, more immediately effective, freer, than any of the preparatory drawings. Around the Virgin and her Son we feel the emotions of a pensive humanity, doubting, distraught, awed, devout, imploring: a whole kaleidoscope of feelings and passions, virtually a complete array of symbols of man's inner activity, of his thirst for knowledge. No work of art, before this painting, had expressed such lofty conceptual content, depicted in such perfect form. Thus the *Adoration* becomes the expression of the human epic, and the first achievement of Leonardo in acquiring a truly universal dimension.

18. Drawing that shows Leonardo's interest in the representation of movement
London, British Museum

19. Drawing of the hanging of Piero Baroncelli
Bayonne, Musée Bonnat

20. Drawing of a rearing horse
Windsor, Royal Library

21

The Adoration

Leonardo was commissioned in 1481 to paint this work for the main altar of the church of San Donato Scopeto, just outside Florence, beyond the Porta a San Piero Gattolino (now called Porta Romana). But the artist never finished the painting and left it behind in Florence when he set out for Milan — as we have seen — in 1481. In a semicircle around the 25 Virgin and Child is the crowd of those who are approaching the Holy Family to worship. There are people of every age, including some young people on horseback. The animals themselves — as was often to happen with Leonardo — seem to share the human emotions. In the background, with the ruins of a palace whose distinct stairs seem almost 24 unreal, a procession of people, mounted and on foot, unfolds. At the extreme right there is an equestrian combat, whose meaning however, remains obscure. The two trees in the center, a palm and an ilex, act almost as the axes around which the whole scene unfolds in a spiral, as if inserted between the meditative figure of an old man on the left and that of a youth (pointing to the group of the 26 Madonna and Child) at the extreme right.

Riderless horses also wander through the paint-

22

23

21. *Adoration of the Magi*
243 x 246 cm.
Florence, Uffizi

22. *Perspective study for the*
Adoration of the Magi
Florence, Uffizi Prints and
Drawings Rooms

23. *Study for the Adoration of*
the Magi
Paris, Louvre

24, 25. *Adoration of the Magi,*
details
Florence, Uffizi

19

ing, perhaps the symbol of a nature not yet subdued by man, while in the background rise the usual high peaks, here barely sketched, but no less solemn and looming than others in Leonardo's work.

26. Adoration of the Magi, detail of the supposed self-portrait
Florence, Uffizi

27. St Jerome
103 x 75 cm
Vatican, Pinacoteca

26

Saint Jerome

27 No contemporary source mentions the *Saint Jerome* in the Vatican Museum, and yet there has never been any doubt concerning the attribution of this panel. The stylistic evidence, linking it with the master's painting methods, is too obvious. Moreover, we have here the formal and structural resemblance (as well as the similarly unfinished
21 state) to the Uffizi *Adoration*, even if the content is clearly different. In the latter we have a throng whose desire for knowledge drives it towards a mystery of universal significance; here we have a solitary hero, his face haggard from fasting and penitence, but his eyes filled with determination and will-power. Leonardo's faces never reflect weak or hesitant feelings: they are steeped in profound passions, revealed, however, not through distortions of the features, but through the intensity of the expression. The head of the Saint, formed through Leonardo's masterly anatomical knowledge, is still part of a Florentine tradition of draftsmanship which, through Antonio del Pollaiolo, extends to

Andrea del Castagno and to Domenico Veneziano. Completely new, summing up the artist's anatomical experiments and the study of movement mentioned above, is the pose of the body, kneeling and bent forward, while the right arm is outstretched, grasping a stone, just before the penitent strikes his breast with it. The figure of the recumbent lion concludes the spiral that surrounds the pyramid represented by the figure of the kneeling Saint. The spiral begins in the mountain of the background, its form familiar by now, then winds around the rocky cave, Jerome's hermitage, to end in the curve of the animal's tail. The structural composition is thus typical of Leonardo. With it, he decidedly abandons the fifteenth-century type of composition, which grouped people and objects symmetrically; now he is moving towards a new concept of volumes and space, more atmospheric and less geometrical. Most critics place this work in Leonardo's first Florentine period, before his departure for Milan.

28. *Drawing of the Madonna suckling the Child and other profiles*
Windsor, Royal Library

Leonardo's women and children

The attraction Leonardo felt towards the beauty of young women and children is demonstrated by numerous drawings. They portray faces sometimes intent, sometimes smiling, attitudes of tender affection, gazes filled with shyness or silent contentment on one hand, and games, childish play, on the other, with delightful children as protagonists. In fact, it is hard to find in the master's work a single-minded interpretation of the female or the childish form, whereas most Quattrocento painters constructed the figure of the Virgin (emblematic of the mother-son relationship) according to unchanging formulas, trying as far as possible to express all feelings connected with that relationship in a kind of regal impassiveness thanks to which the Virgin can be only the Child's worshiper. Instead, Leonardo's typical way of facing human situations, namely through minute analysis of the emotional and physiological elements that form them, finds also in the subject of the "Madonna and Child" a further possibility of expression.

A different kind of emotional relationship is al-

24

32 ready being expressed in the so-called *Benois Madonna* in the Hermitage Museum, Leningrad. Here a very young Madonna, hardly more than a girl, is seen playing with her Son, showing him a flower. The girl is conscious of her action and smiles, while the child, who must still examine the object his mother has held out to him, seems grave, intent on observing it. These nuances of feeling show us how Leonardo succeeded in achieving, in painting, his private program of study of the human figure and of its physical components and its behavior. Naturally Leonardo's interest in the female figure cannot be limited to the subject dealt with here: there are also female portraits by Leonardo (which culminate, obviously, in the world-famous *Gioconda*). One of them is the now firmly identified 70 portrait of *Ginevra Benci* in the National Gallery 66 in Washington, a work which can rightfully be considered the prototype of this genre of painting, even if it is stylistically still linked, in many ways, with late fifteenth-century Florentine painting and, especially, with the products of Verrocchio's shop. In any case, this is a work which also betrays Leonardo's efforts to insert the human figure into nature, an enterprise which — as we have seen — concerned him from his beginnings as an artist. Here we witness a first stage of this enterprise, where nature assumes the function of a background which puts the woman's figure in relief. She is not outstandingly beautiful, but her expression is intense, and her face

30. Drawing of the Madonna
and Child holding a cat
London, British Museum

31. Domenico Ghirlandaio
Birth of St John the Baptist,
detail
Florence, Santa Maria Novella

reveals a mixed feeling of pride and melancholy. The splendid evergreen bough that rises behind the figure has — if observed carefully — an autonomy of its own, both because of its relevance in the work's context and because of the loving care with which it was painted, although it is not possible to identify absolutely the species of tree. What is most striking is this female face whose penetrating gaze seems to ennoble the simple geometric form which traces its outline. We are spontaneously led to comparisons with the dignified but banal ladies in the

31 domestic processions of Domenico Ghirlandaio's

fresco cycles, painted almost at the same time as these early works of Leonardo. The comparison offers a further confirmation of the greater complexity and superior quality of the artistic program of the youth from Vinci. The so-called *Litta Madonna*, also now in the Hermitage in Leningrad, has been assigned by scholars to the Milan period. A drawing exists which is definitely related to this painting, but the painting nevertheless is most likely the work of a follower. In the painting the Virgin's attitude is more markedly affectionate; there is a tenderness and satisfaction in the contemplation of the Child,

33

31

who, intent on sucking his mother's milk, looks towards the imagined observer. This painting resumes the traditional theme of the "nursing Madonna" enriching it, however, with attentive observation of the Child. The somatic type of the infant Jesus is already the same as the one we will later see 35 in the *Virgin of the Rocks* and in the *Saint Anne*: a 72 blond, curly-haired baby, with very delicate complexion. In conclusion, we may observe that this

beauty expressed in the soft forms of young Madonnas and the plump features of the Infants is, in Leonardo, something more than mere figurative representation. It is a speculation on the concept of maternity, seen in the emotional relationship with the child and entrusted to the instrument of painting, which in that very beauty finds its appropriate expression.

The Benois Madonna and Litta Madonna

32 The first of these works was originally painted on wood and was transferred to canvas when it entered the Hermitage. The painting was not discovered by scholars until it was shown along with other works from private collections in St. Petersburg in 1909; its provenance is unknown. Only its Russian history is documented: it was acquired by Tsar Nicholas II in 1914. The attribution to Leonardo was immediate and almost unanimous. The Virgin's fresh beauty and the Child's intense expression, as he looks at the flower his mother gives him, are noteworthy. These are perhaps the first figures conceived and realized by Leonardo in complete formal and stylistic independence of his

master's shop, though still in his Florentine period. The work can be roughly dated somewhere between 1475 and 1480.

The *Litta Madonna*, on the other hand, belongs 33 to the Milanese period; the Lombard elements in it are evident: a realistic care in the painting of the drapery and a general tone of domestic intimacy. This painting, which passed from the hands of the Visconti to the Litta family, was also purchased by a Tsar. The Emperor Alexander II, in 1865, added it to the Hermitage, where it was transferred to canvas. Recent scholarship tends to consider this a work by Leonardo completed by Boltraffio, one of his Milanese pupils.

27

32

33

32. *Benois Madonna*
48 x 31 cm
Leningrad, Hermitage

33. *Litta Madonna*
42 x 33 cm
Leningrad, Hermitage

34. Madonna of the Carnation
62 x 47 cm
Munich, Alte Pinakothek

The Madonna of the Carnation

Another work that would seem to evoke the sketches of a young Leonardo freed from Verrrocchio's tutelage, though nevertheless still affected by a passion and taste for the soft textures and dazzle ·of solid material (as practised in the workshop of the Florentine artist), is the Madonna sometimes referred to as the *Madonna of the Carnation* or "Madonna of the flowers". This painting is a free variant of the *Benois Madonna* in the Hermitage, being more complex in its composition and spatial arrangement, though perhaps somewhat high-flown and less spontaneous. How it arrived at the Alte Pinakothek in Munich, after its acquisition by a private German collector, is unknown to us. What is certain is that after a comprehensible, temporary attribution to Verrocchio or his shop, art critics subsequently almost universally assigned the painting to Leonardo, a judgement backed up by the most recent research. In fact, the richness of the drapery, the vastness of the mountain scenery with purple and gold hues tinging the foothills of peaks that fade into the sky, the vitality of the cut flowers in the crystal vase and the softness of the Child's flesh that foreshadows the tender putti of the *Virgin of the Rocks*, are elements that show a distancing from the more distinctive Verrocchiesque style and instead assume those formal and chromatic characteristics that would be the mature Leonardo's very own. Moreover, we should not overlook the striking similarities — in facial features and other details — with the *Benois Madonna* already mentioned (the gem fastening the Virgin's gown over her breast) and with the Uffizi *Annunciation*, works that in their figurative and expressive invention quite clearly reveal the stamp of Leonardo.

The Virgin of the Rocks in the Louvre

The first work that Leonardo executed in Milan is the so-called *Virgin of the Rocks*, which actually expresses the theme of the Immaculate Conception, the dogma that affirms Christ was conceived without original sin on Mary's part. This canvas was to decorate the ancona (a carved wooden altar with frames where paintings were inserted) in the chapel of the Immacolata in the church of San Francesco Grande in Milan. On 25 April 1483, the members of the Confraternity of the Conception assigned the work of the paintings (a Virgin and Child in the center and two Angel-Musicians for the sides), to Leonardo, for the most important part, and the brothers Ambrogio and Evangelista De Predis, for the side panels. Scholars now feel that the two canvases on this same subject, one in the Louvre and the other in London's National Gallery, are simply two versions of the same painting, with significant variants.

The Paris *Virgin of the Rocks*, entirely by Leonardo, is the one which first adorned the altar in San Francesco Grande. It may have been given by Leonardo himself to King Louis XII of France, in gratitude for the settlement of the suit between the painters and those who commissioned the works, in dispute over the question of payment. The later London painting replaced this one in the ancona. For the first time Leonardo could achieve in painting that intellectual program of fusion between human forms and nature which was slowly taking shape in his view of his art. Here there are no thrones or architectural structures to afford a spatial frame for the figures; instead there are the rocks of a grotto, reflected in limpid waters, decorated by leaves of various kinds from different plants while in the distance, as if emerging from a mist composed of very fine droplets and filtered by the golden sunlight, the peaks of those mountains we now know so well reappear. This same light reveals the gentle, mild features of the Madonna, the angel's smiling face, the plump, pink flesh of the two putti. For this work, too, Leonardo made numerous studies, and the figurative expression is slowly adapted to the program of depiction. In fact, the drawing of the face of the angel is, in the sketch, clearly feminine, with a fascination that has nothing ambiguous about it. In the painting, the sex is not defined, and the angel could easily be either a youth or a maiden.

35

35. Virgin of the Rocks
198 x 123 cm
Paris, Louvre

36. Drawing of the face of the angel from the Virgin of the Rocks
Turin, National Library

37, 38. Drawings of plants and rocks, probable studies for the Virgin of the Rocks
Windsor, Royal Library

36

37

38

33

39, 40. Virgin of the Rocks, details
Paris, Louvre

The Virgin of the Rocks in the London National Gallery

43 This version of the painting for the ancona in San Francesco has distinctly sixteenth-century characteristics: larger figures, made more plastic by a very decided chiaroscuro so unlike Leonardo that scholars were immediately led to consider the work a collaboration. The canvas is generally considered the one that replaced the first version of the Virgin of the Rocks on the altar of the Immaculate Conception, after that version had been given to Louis XII. This version was then, in 1785, purchased by the English collector Gavin Hamilton. It was joined, in England, in 1898, by the two musician-angels of the De Predis brothers, and the three paintings are now displayed together in London's National Gallery.

This version shows some details generally neglected by Leonardo in the other version: the haloes of the figures, the child Saint John's cross of reeds. Other elements which differ from the Paris picture are the pose of the angel, who no longer points his finger towards the little Paraclete, and his face, whose gaze no longer seeks out the spectator, but is directed inwards. The drapery, too, which in the Paris version was heavy and concealed the body, is lighter here, revealing the anatomical structure. Also the rocks seem painted in a more plastic fashion; the light does not glide over them, creating dewy areas of semi-darkness, but leaves strong contrasts of light and dark. The flesh of the children here is less tender, and though the shadows are insistent, the children's faces seem flatter and less sweet than those of the two sublime creatures in Paris. The intervention of followers on the painting already sketched by Leonardo has made the portrayal less vibrant, more banal, though it retains a compositional authority and an originality in its variants that make this work not a copy but an autonomous version, of high quality, of the unequalled masterpiece in the Louvre.

41, 42. Child from the Paris and London Virgin of the Rocks, details

43. Virgin of the Rocks
189.5 x 120 cm
London, National Gallery

41

42

44

Leonardo in Milan

Leonardo's first stay in Milan (1482-1499) in the period of his life most rich in activity, are the years that made his name and his personality well-known throughout Italy. During this time he undertook his largest number of important works, some completed, some left unfinished, some merely conceived or sketched. This is the moment when his art takes that firmly autonomous direction which, begun with 21 the *Adoration of the Magi*, found in Milan its conformation, so that the style seen in his paintings was no longer based on "Florentine" or "Lombard" formulas, but was a Leonardesque style, later to have its own emulators, followers, and imitators.

As we have mentioned before, Leonardo seized the opportunity of Lorenzo the Magnificent's willingness to send artists to the various Italian states. He came to the Lombard capital, then perhaps Italy's most important city for its geographical position, wealth of industry, and political power. It also had a fertile populous territory, while Milan itself was a humanistic center filled with cultural ferment, even if it could not rival the refinement and creative ca-

pacity of the Florence of the Medici. In the famous letter to the Duke of Milan, Leonardo insisted on his abilities as an artist, and clearly hinted at an undertaking which must have been very dear to Sforza, namely the "construction of a bronze horse, which will be to the immortal glory and eternal honor of your father [Francesco I] and to the illustrious House of Sforza".

But when it came to the execution of this equestrian monument there was no lack of problems and hesitancy both on the part of the patron and of the master. Leonardo was troubled by the constant modifications of the original project, an ambitious group of dimensions never seen before (about 7.20 meters in height), with a rearing horse which presented difficulties of equilibrium and of casting. The Duke began gradually to harbor doubts concerning Leonardo's ability to execute the work, and in 1490 he wrote again to Lorenzo the Magnificent, asking for Florentine masters expert in casting bronze equestrian statues. Perhaps spurred on by this demonstration of his patron's lack of confidence

44. *Study for the Sforza monument*
Windsor, Royal Library

45. *Study for the Trivulzio monument*
Windsor, Royal Library

46. *Last Supper*
460 x 880 cm
Milan, Santa Maria delle Grazie

45

in him, Leonardo went back to work, and in 1491 he seemed to have made good progress, according to his own account. But then more doubts arose about the casting in bronze and the work's definitive appearance. We know that in 1498 a clay model was ready and the projects for the casting had already reached an advanced stage. In fact, the techniques worked out by Leonardo were later to be used by other artists. These techniques won him the reputation of being a precursor, an aspect of his work which modern writers have particularly accentuated. By a quirk of fate, Leonardo was unable to carry out this gigantic, tormented work according to his artistic meditations and his painfully acquired knowledge of the techniques of casting. In 1499 the Duchy of Milan was invaded by French troops un-der Louis XII. The Duke fled, and the model of the Sforza monument was consequently destroyed. Countless drawings of it remain: poses, attitudes, anatomies of horses, which show how Leonardo also dissected and studied these animals, with the spirit both of a scientist and an artist; there are also some sketches regarding casting techniques, with captions. A dejected annotation in one of Leonardo's notebooks, with the melancholy title *Epitaph*, perhaps concludes the artist's labors on this work: *If I have been unable to do, if I...* This unfinished sentence seems truly intended to underline the master's dazed disappointment at the failure to carry out another work of his.

We have already discussed the *Virgin of the Rocks* in its two versions, in London and Paris. We

44

35

43

39

47

47. *Study for the head of James from the Last Supper*
Windsor, Royal Library

48. *Last Supper, detail*
Milan, Santa Maria delle Grazie

various artistic techniques (it has been reproduced on tapestries, engraved, carved in wood). The literary references are meaningful, both for their quantity and quality. The fresco is mentioned by poets and historians, beginning with Matteo Bandello, almost a contemporary, in the dedication of the fifty-eighth Novella of the first part of his collection, and continuing through Goethe, who described it, after he had seen it in May, 1788. No other work, finally, has aroused greater public concern over its preservation and its restoration. It began to deteriorate rapidly soon after it was completed, and already by Vasari's time (1568) it could hardly be deciphered. The restorations were nearly all unfortunate, to tell the truth, except for the most recent ones, under the guidance of Mauro Pellicioli, which have actually made some recovery possible, such as the surface of the table and the figure of Judas. The earlier attempts contributed to worsening the appearance of the work, beginning in the eighteenth century and involving the various administrations which followed one another in the government of the city of Milan (first the Austrians, then the newly-born Kingdom of Italy, at the end of the last century). This itinerary of interventions is indicative of the fresco. In fact, it holds the fascination of a superb measure of content and form, perhaps never achieved again absolutely, except in some frescoes in Raphael's Rooms in the Vatican, where, for that matter, the illustrative effect is more dominant. The action in the *Last Supper* is choral: Christ's words pass, like a gust of impetuous wind, over the assembled disciples, who comment, in groups of three, on the Master's overwhelming revelation: "One of you shall betray me" (Matthew, XXVI, 21). It is as if the serenity of this room, classical in its architecture and its proportions, were suddenly destroyed, and among those present the knowledge is circulating of a tragedy that will soon be fulfilled, inevitably. Beyond the three openings in the back, a very clear, late-summer afternoon sky is the natural note Leonardo introduces into the depiction of an essentially human drama, fusing it, however, in supreme harmony with the surrounding atmosphere. Years of plans, countless preparatory drawings revealing differing compositional solutions are the prelude to the execution of this masterpiece, which was —

must add that the vicissitudes of this repeated panel were far from serene. There were endless disputes which set the patrons, the members of the Company of the Conception of San Francesco Grande, against Leonardo and the De Predis brothers, the artists of the works that were to decorate the altar of the chapel of the Immacolata in that same church. The Paris version is now in the Louvre precisely because King Louis XII personally intervened to settle the argument, and Leonardo probably gave him the painting out of gratitude for his arbitration. In any case, it is the first real painting Leonardo produced in Milan. However, far more tormented in its genesis and also the most significant work Leonardo ever painted — at least among those that have survived and are certainly his — is the painting that followed the *Virgin of the Rocks*, namely the *Last Supper* in Santa Maria delle Grazie. Probably no work of art has taken on the universal character that this fresco has, though it is now only a pale shadow of what it must have been when the master's hand had just completed it. It is of immense artistic and religious importance. Protestants and Catholics alike have accepted, without hesitation, the fact that it represents — and we know copies and imitations made for both religious areas — the central point of the Christian doctrine of salvation, the institution of the Eucharist during the Passover supper celebrated by Christ and his disciples together.

In fact, there are numerous versions and derivations of the fresco in every field of art and even in

46

42

again according to Bandello — characterized by alternating phases of execution: whole days of intense application, then a few minutes of rapid brush-strokes. This account may give an idea of the trepidation with which Leonardocarried out the most demanding work he had ever undertaken. His immense spiritual and technical engagement has left still visible marks in the painting, which, though veiled in the colors and the volumes of the figures, makes a profound impression even today and allows us to understand the grandeur and the originality of Leonardo's creation.

Compared with the *Last Supper*, the other works executed by Leonardo during his Milanese period take second place, though they represent a vast and various production also as far as subject and genre are concerned. Closely connected with Leonardo's life and activity as a courtier is the decoration of the so-called Sala delle Asse in the Castello Sforzesco. Some traces of the decoration were discovered during the 1893 restoration. It is an exceptional interlacing of branches of trees, with ropes, leaving only some patches of sky visible; they start at the beginning of the vault and form a kind of arbor with greenery, the coat-of-arms of Lodovico Sforza appearing in the center. The present state of the decoration is that given it during the late nineteenth-century renovation; but the idea, in its naturalistic vitality, can be assigned to Leonardo, while the execution of these ornamental paintings was surely the work of his disciples. His court activity also involved him in stage designing, in the organizing and staging of ceremonies (such as the receptions and festivities on the occasion of Gian Galeazzo Sforza's marriage to Isabella of Aragon in 1490). At the same time Leonardo had to attend to the execution of his reclamation project, demanded by Sforza for his landholdings near Vigevano, thus putting to the test his talents as a hydraulic engineer of which he himself boasted in his letter to Lodovico. Moreover, as we have seen, he was constantly occupied with the problems of casting the monument to Francesco Sforza and he also painted (if the attributions of the majority of Leonardo scholars and critics are correct) some portraits of personages who for one reason or another were connected with the Sforza court. We will discuss these at greater length below.

In short, Leonardo was continuously occupied, and his work served also to increase enormously his already exceptional reputation.

The last work executed by Leonardo before the King of France and his troops invaded the city and the artist left it (1499), is the cartoon for the *Madonna and Child with Saint Anne*, now in the National Gallery, London. The cartoon is of exceptional importance because of the influence on Italian painting in the early sixteenth century of the pyramidal composition of the figures portrayed in it. But, in itself, the work is a unique example of formal beauty, compositional harmony, and profound conceptual significance. It is the logical conclusion of a complex investigation into the capacity of painting to reveal human feelings without upsetting the balance of forms which must be at the base of every experience. From the modulated, yet harmonic figures of the disciples, who start at the words of their Master in the *Last Supper*, to this compact group of the *Saint Anne*, where the faces seem to communicate to one another the feelings of the spirit (and, at least in our view, not reciprocally eluding one another, as some critics have thought), Leonardo's formal discourse is coherent and progressive.

In Milan, finally, he drew around him a group of followers and pupils (this is the final consideration we would like to make in this part of our discussion), such as Melzi, Marco d'Oggiono, Cesare da Sesto, Boltraffio, Salaino, and many others. He treated them with almost paternal generosity and affection, as we can see directly from his notebooks, indulgent even when their behavior could provoke severe reactions and punishments. (This was the case with Salaino, a youth of great beauty, but bizarre and full of all sorts of character defects). Intense work and affectionate ties are thus the chief characteristics of Leonardo's first Milanese period, perhaps the most important period — as we have tried to indicate — of his life as a scientist, artist, and man.

49. *Last Supper, detail*
Milan, Santa Maria delle Grazie

50

The Last Supper

The Duke Lodovico chose the Dominican church of Santa Maria delle Grazie both as his family chapel and burial-palace. In 1492 he had Bramante create a new choir in the form of a cube crowned by a dome and (perhaps in 1494) he commissioned 46 Leonardo to paint the *Last Supper*. The painting was to occupy the north wall of the refectory, and Leonardo spent more than three years working on preparatory studies, sketches, and drawings. The Franciscan monk Luca Pacioli of Borgo Sansepolcro, mathematician and friend of the artist, in his dedication of the treatise *De divina proportione* to Lodovico, dated 8 February 1498, states that he saw the work completed. So Leonardo must have devoted himself to it from 1495 to 1498. The theme of the Cenacle, or Last Supper, is as old as Christian art itself, but it was only with conventual painting that it became the typical subject for the refectories of monasteries, where as a rule it was depicted in mural paintings of vast proportions. In the first preparatory drawings, Leonardo seems to want to

accept the traditional scheme, with Judas — the traitor — seated opposite Christ. But, already at the beginning, "his conception of the theme was completely dominated by the idea of portraying the announcement of the betrayal as the central dramatic motive" (Heydenreich). In Leonardo's conception of the Last Supper, then, it is the human aspect of the drama being fulfilled which predominates, and not the sacred and mystical moment of the actual institution of the Eucharist, when Christ, taking the bread and the chalice, offers them to the disciples, saying: "Take, eat..." (Mark, XIV, 22-23). In the execution of the painting, Judas is seated on the

50. Study for the Last Supper
Venice, Academy

51. Last Supper, detail
Milan, Santa Maria delle Grazie

46

51

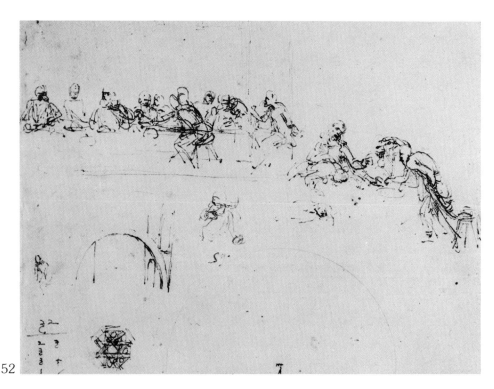

52. *Study for the Last Supper*
Windsor, Royal Library

53. *Study of horses' hind*
quarters
Windsor, Royal Library

54. *Study of the proportions of*
the human head
Venice, Academy

same side of the table as Christ and the other disciples. Only his attitude sharply distinguishes him from the others, as they echo the Master's words. As all, in fact, either lean towards Jesus or comment, aghast, on his revelation, Judas seems to detach himself purposely from the common drama, remaining isolated and ambiguous, with the burden of his betrayal. The unusual arrangement of the people is not the only novelty in Leonardo's fresco; also new is his identification, not entrusted to titles with the respective names, but rather to a complex of visual indications, which the gospel tradition and subsequent hagiography have handed down to posterity (particular function within the apostolic community, kinship, martyrology, attitudes towards the Master, and so on). And, naturally, the pictorial technique itself was entirely new, now surpassing fifteenth-century painting to express a far more complex sense of atmosphere, surroundings and color.

The masterpiece became immediately famous and popular with the public. Some sources report a significant tradition: the French King Francis I supposedly wanted to have the whole wall on which the *Last Supper* is painted sawn off and taken to France. Another historical fact is the painting's survival in 1943 when Allied bombs destroyed the ceiling of the refectory and almost the entire apse of Santa Maria delle Grazie. The painting's very poor state of preservation, which makes us regret the fact that we are unable to enjoy it completely, was attributed by certain historians (including Vasari) to the technique used by Leonardo. More recent restorations and a careful reading of the sources have proved instead that the painting's deterioration is due to the humidity which has always impregnated the wall and the entire refectory. But, beyond its present condition, Leonardo's idea and his achievement survive, giving this drama a truly universal scope and meaning.

3

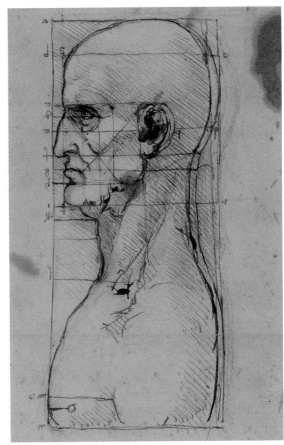

54

Anatomy, mechanics, caricature

"The ancients called man the lesser world, and truly this expression is well-founded, for as man is made up of earth, water, air, and fire, this body is a resemblance to the earth".

This sentence of Leonardo's may furnish the key to an interpretation of his concept of the world and of man, seen not only in strict interdependence, but actually similarly structured, and therefore capable of being studied with the same means. From the beginning of his career as an artist, he was an alert observer not only of landscapes but also of the traces of telluric upheavals which caused the earth's conformation (the view of the *Gonfolina Strait*, where the Arno's flow narrows before the river opens out in the lower valley, dates from 15 August 1473); and similarly, the artist observed man in his interior structure to which the exterior corresponds, physical aspect, physiognomy, expression of feelings, movement — all is minutely dissected, in order to discover the secret mechanism that governs man's vitality. The inner workings of the sensations of sight and hearing, the physiological instruments by which man can make his voice heard, the arrange-

ment of muscles enabling movement: these are the most important themes of Leonardo's anatomical research. The many anatomical drawings which he left behind, however, are not cold, didactic compositions; always present in them is that supreme quality which characterizes the master's works, so that even these scientific exercises have an independent artistic value, like every other creation of Leonardo's. We must bear in mind that the studies for the *Adoration of the Magi* and the *Last Supper* were made from naked figures, whose anatomy was carefully delineated. This method, which was to find followers from Cinquecento painting on, was actually begun by Leonardo. But man is not merely adorned with handsome features; in his life there is not only youth, marked by delicate complexion and perfect lineaments. Old age also exists, with its wrinkles and its deformities; ugliness exists, with its unpleasant and even repulsive features. Leonardo has therefore recorded the presence of deformity in man. We are told he visited the most ill-famed quarters of Milan, to draw the faces of those whose bodies and spirits had been in-

55. Study of the proportions of the human body
Venice, Academy

56. Drawing of the assembly of a cannon
Windsor, Royal Library

57. Drawing of an assault chariot with scythes
Turin, National Library

58. Study of a man's head
Venice, Academy

59. Study of an old man's profile
Firenze, Uffizi Prints and Drawings Rooms

56

57

58

59

60. Drawing of grotesque heads
Windsor, Royal Library

61. Study of caricatures
Venice, Academy

delibly marked by poverty and vice. But we can also believe that this "underlining" in the negative sense, this distortion of man's features derives from the idea that both good and evil are part of humanity. They are not, however, considered in a moralistic sense, but simply represented as objective facts. For Leonardo, after all, the exercise of his art was also a philosophical speculation: "Painting then is philosophy... because it deals with the motion of bodies in the promptness of their actions, and philosophy is also a part of motion...".

Once the workings of human and natural organisms are known, they can be reproduced in machines which help man take his place in the world, encouraging his ambitions and his dreams of power. From the time of his study with Verrocchio, Leonardo was introduced to the learning of the "artes mechanicae, which had its natural seat in the shops of artists... an apprenticeship far more vast and eclectic [than mere artistic teaching] which was to produce an engineer or rather a technician-artist who could be called upon... to build a church, a

palace, a fortress, war machines, bridges, dykes, and canals" (Marinoni). Thus we have Leonardo's letter to Lodovico Il Moro, where he lists his talents as a civil and military engineer (as well as his gifts as a musician and artist, naturally), a list compiled in order to whet the Duke's appetites in his war-plans. So there are a whole series of sketches and studies for war machines, immense catapults, cannon with multiple barrels, grapeshot mortars, projectiles whose form suggests that of the lethal instruments of death of our own time. And, parallel to these, studies of civil engineering and mechanics: bridges, spinning machines, locks, watermills, compasses, springs, embankments, gears, even a vehicle amazingly like our modern bicycle. These remarks on Leonardo's studies of anatomy, physiognomy, and mechanics can help us understand the systematic foundation, the unity of the thought and activity of this great scientist, philosopher, and artist. In the past, critics tended to underline or exalt one or the other aspect of this complex personality, ignoring his constant coherence.

56
57

62. Study of the heads of an old man and a youth
Florence, Uffizi Prints and Drawings Rooms

The portraits

Among Leonardo's activities as a painter during his first stay in Milan we must include his portraits, which several sources mention clearly. The problem was one of identifying (not following the documents, which lack information and are very uncertain on the subject, but rather working from stylistic analysis) a certain number of portraits which could conform to Leonardo's figurative tendencies in this period. It must be said that the Lombard tradition of portraiture was quite distinct from the Florentine. The latter was celebratory and, in some instances, synthetic (even the so-called *Ginevra Benci*, for all its undeniably novel characteristics, also possesses these qualities), whereas Lombard portraiture was realistic, analytical, paying attention to style of dress, coiffure, and to accessory elements in general. Moreover the presence of Antonello da Messina in the Po Valley (he was in Venice in 1475) helped spread a certain kind of portraiture, with the figure against a dark ground and with a careful depiction of expressions and attitudes. In the works that scholars have indicated as possible paintings by Leonardo we can observe common characteristics, such as the background left in shadow, the figure seen at half-length or slightly more, in a three-quarters turn to enable the observer to distinguish the sitter more easily. The subjects of the portraits, however, remain unidentified, despite all the efforts of art historians and interpreters of the documents concerning Leonardo's activity. We can unquestionably place Leonardo's portraits in the circle of the Sforza court, where obviously what counted was the celebration of the individual, coinciding with that of the court itself. Clarity of forms, dignity of attitude, but at the same time an acute penetration of the character of the subject: in the portraits Leonardo immediately aligns his art with what we might call the avant-garde in this sort of painting, namely the portraiture of Antonello da Messina, definitively surpassing the celebratory formalism of the fifteenth century and heading decisively towards the figure of man depicted in the spiritual state that best defines him.

The subject of the so-called *Portrait of a Musician* in the Ambrosiana in Milan was at one time identified as Franchino Gaffurio, "maestro di cappella" of the Milanese cathedral; but the work actually appears simply as the portrait of a young man holding a length of paper with some musical annotation on it. The work can still suggest some geometrical volumes of Tuscan origin: the cap and the mass of curly hair which form two hemispheres at the sides of the face; but the incisiveness of the features and the chiaroscuro immediately suggest the Lombard atmosphere and a knowledge of Antonello's portraits. Heavily restored and repainted, the work was probably left unfinished, though at an advanced stage. This portrait — if it is by Leonardo — is the only one of the artist's with a male subject. It reveals a decisive personality, an intelligent and resolute gaze. No forced poses, therefore, aimed at a bombastic celebration of the sitter, but rather a depiction of moral strength through the intrinsic light of the face and the gaze. Antonello's lesson was learned and applied with a superior technique, showing that in Leonardo's sphere any artistic tendency could find affirmation and further development.

The second portrait of the Milanese group attributed to Leonardo is the *Lady with an Ermine*, now in the Czartoryski Gallery in Cracow, Poland. This is a remarkable portrayal of a slender maiden, with a faint smile and a penetrating gaze, holding in her arms a little white animal, gently pressing it with her agile, tapering hand. A transparent cap which passes beneath her chin softens the oval of the face, while a simple necklace of dark pearls, in two loops around her neck and extending in two strands over her bosom, barely suggested by the square-cut dress, is her only ornament. Her large, intent eyes are prominent, her nose is straight and fine, and her little mouth with thin lips is almost imperceptibly parted at the corners in a faint smile. Also remarkable is the handling of the fur of the animal, painted with a tiny paw upraised. The white color of this fur has caused the animal to be identified as an ermine in its winter coat, a symbol of purity. Despite some doubts about the identity of the subject, there is an hypothesis that she is Cecilia Gallerani, the favorite of Ludovico il Moro up to his wedding. The girl is recalled, in fact, as a friend of Leonardo's, who must, in fact, have painted her at the Sforza court, according to information from contemporary sources. Though the work has been so repainted that it is impossibile to attribute it definitively, the

63. Portrait of Isabella d'Este
63 x 46 cm
Paris, Louvre

57

64

state of preservation of the girl's face and of the ermine is fair, and can demonstrate the presence of a very notable technique and a skill of execution which can only belong to the environment of Leonardo, and to his immediate circle.

64. *Portrait of a Musician*
43 x 31 cm
Milan, Pinacoteca Ambrosiana

65. *Lady with an Ermine*
54 x 39 cm
Cracow, Czartoryski Museum

65

66

Ginevra Benci

This panel, now in the National Gallery, Washington, portrays a young woman against a landscape with trees, illuminated by the glints of a stream. There are conflicting opinions as to the identity of the subject, and scholars similarly are not in agreement about the date of the work. Some feel that it belongs to the first Florentine period; others assign it to the Milanese years. In any case, the most generally accepted view is that the sitter is Ginevra Benci (a juniper — "ginepro" — branch, painted on the back of the panel, suggests her name), and that the work dates from the period when Leonardo was freeing himself from Verrocchio's tutelage — around 1475.

66. *Ginevra Benci*
42 x 37 cm
Washington, National Gallery

67. *Copy from Leonardo, Leda*
Rome, Galleria Borghese

68. *Study for the hair of Leda*
Windsor, Royal Library

The smile in Leonardo

Perhaps the greatest, most widespread interest in any of Leonardo's works is that which everywhere and at all times has been concentrated on the *Gioconda's* smile. Actually, other characters of Leonardo have the same smile — subtle and ironic, lips pressed together — as the protagonist of this famous canvas in Paris. The figures of the Virgin and Saint Anne in the cartoon and in the panel of the same title, for example, have it; and so does the *Leda*, which does not survive in the Master's version, though its derivative versions show an indisputable fidelity to Leonardo's model; and there is the mysterious, chiaroscuro *Baptist*. Leonardo's seal, you might say, has been imprinted on the face of each of these figures thanks to that smile which has noth-

ing ambiguous about it, but still leaves us a bit perplexed because of its allusive hint of irony. This sort of smile — from a figurative point of view — was not invented by Leonardo. It can be found in certain fifteenth-century Florentine sculptures, such as Antonio Rossellino's *Virgin* in the marble tondo of the Portuguese Cardinal's chapel in San Miniato al Monte, and much more widely in the works of Leonardo's master, Verrocchio. In these instances the smile has a specific function: to enliven, in a pictorial sense, the renewed sculpture of the Renaissance, whose founder Donatello had given it a severe and heroic form. But Leonardo, while surely inspired by that sculpture, takes his smile from there to give it quite a different function and meaning. In

61

it we may truly say that Leonardo's progress through the contents of painting is concluded. From the portrayal of childhood and maternal sentiment in the youthful *Madonnas*, to the moods and movement of the *Adoration*, to the dramatic and choral synthesis of the *Last Supper*, he reaches a reconsideration of the individual personality in the *portraits*. At this point Leonardo had to find the formal expression of man's attitude towards the world around him, towards that nature which, though investigated with such attention, still remains largely secret. This mixed feeling of confidence and uncertainty can only be expressed in the face: and expression in the face is the smile. Not a total smile, of irresistible joy or hilarity, for that would not express the doubts hidden in the human spirit; but rather a smile filled with irony and intelligence, aware of the boundaries of human knowledge; a smile, finally, where Leonardo's concept of the world is reflected in its entirety. And in this limited expression of human feeling the artist succeeds in synthesizing man's attitude towards what is around him: a universal expression, therefore, since it is largely valid even today.

The cartoon with Saint Anne

Drawn in charcoal with touches of paint, this cartoon is now in the National Gallery in London, moved there in 1966 from the Royal Academy, which had owned it at least since 1791. In 1763 the cartoon had been bought in Venice from the Sagredo family by the brother of the English ambassador resident there, Robert Udny. Critics seem to agree on the date of 1498 for the work, at the end of Leonardo's first period in Milan. The group is conceived and realized in a single block, where varying emotions are, however, concentrated, thus inspiring different interpretations of the work. The concatenation of emotions is reflected immediately in the attitudes of the figures, all of them possessing an inner movement, so that the whole group seems to rotate and to communicate, in this writhing, the intensity of the feelings it expresses. Saint Anne's energy, the Virgin's heartfelt sweetness, the Child's grave awareness and the devoted attention of the young Baptist find their synthesis in the compactness of the pyramidal composition. No painting was made from this cartoon. Bernardino Luini, adding Saint Joseph, painted a canvas from it, the *Holy Family*, now in the Pinacoteca Ambrosiana, Milan.

69. Cartoon with St Anne
159 x 101 cm
London, National Gallery

La Gioconda

46 Only the fame of the *Last Supper*, as we have seen, can be compared with that of this portrait, unconditionally celebrated for centuries. After painting it, Leonardo kept it for himself; then it passed directly to Francis I of France, and from him to the Louvre Museum, where it remains today. Scholars generally feel it was painted in Florence around 1503, but there is little agreement about the identity of the subject. Many critics accept the tradition, based on

70 Vasari's report, that the sitter is *Monna Lisa*, wife of Francesco del Giocondo, a Florentine citizen. We must add, however, that this identification clashes with other, later observations of the painting. Since definitive documentation is lacking, in any case, a tradition with the authority of centuries behind it may be safely considered. The portrait's structure surpasses, in one bound, the Antonello scheme noted in earlier works in the genre. Here the subject is seen at half-length, seated, slightly turned, gazing towards the spectator. The background is no longer a darkness against which the figure stands out sharply; instead we have a landscape, "unreal and dream-like, and yet precise as a map... steeped in dampness and dissolved mists" (Ottino Della Chiesa). This is certainly the synthesis of Leonardo's landscape and topographical studies, carried out also for public works (the project for altering the course of the Arno with a canal, and the consequent flooding of the Valdichiana, led the artist to draw many maps of the region between the Tyrrhenian Sea and the Appenines). The fascination of this painting, apart from the familiar observations on the mystery of the smile and the charm of the young woman, is all too well-known and has given rise to hundreds of fantastic hypotheses. We can definitely state, however, that its true fascination lies in the perfect correspondence of expression between the person portrayed and the nature which serves as background, achieved by the "sfumato" technique. The unquestionable sense of irony in the young woman's face, which becomes a universal view of man's attitude towards nature, is thus fused with the execution of the landscape, synthesizing the grandeur of a world that man is in the process of discovering and interpreting. But much is still left unexpressed, in mystery. Leonardo therefore overcomes the eternal dilemma between the idea and its realization, because he places painting at the service of his conceptual meditations, and painting is at once an expressive and a visualizing medium. Moreover, moment by moment, he checks his pictorial technique against his concept of the world: "The image, before reaching the painter's hands, must undergo a long gestation in his spirit" (Marinoni). We can rightly say, in conclusion, that in the execution of *La Gioconda*, Leonardo succeeds in expressing fully this higher demand of his intellect and of his art. This harmony endows the work with its greatness and value.

70. La Gioconda
77 x 53 cm
Paris, Louvre

71

Saint Anne

On the subject of the Virgin and Child with Saint Anne Leonardo had already reflected in his Milanese period, when he prepared the cartoon with these figures, now in the National Gallery in London. But, as we said above, he never translated this cartoon into a painting. The painting we are considering here is neither a version nor a derivation of that earlier idea. Here the structure is autonomous, and also the conceptual significance differs considerably. Against the background of a circle of mountains emerging from mists, as if they were painfully taking shape from the chaos before the Creation, there rises the pyramidal group of Saint Anne, the Virgin, and the Infant Jesus, with a lamb, the symbol of his future sacrifice. The barely perceptible smiles of the faces are the only expression of feeling in the whole painting, which is actually an anthology of very beautiful parts (the mountains, the holy group, the tree on the right), not closely related to one another. We are far from the vibrant, loving colloquy of the London cartoon; still, in the tense movement of the Madonna, drawing the Child towards her, as he seems to want to elude her and play with the lamb, we find a typical Leonardo element, the depiction of movement closely involved in the structure of the group: a conceptual invention of extraordinary originality which did not fail to inspire later artists.

The work, unfinished, was almost certainly executed by Leonardo with the assistance of pupils during his stay in Florence in 1508, when he was commissioned to paint the panel for the main altar of the Santissima Annunziata. This painting, along with the notebooks and other works, went to Francesco Melzi when the master died. It was found by the French in 1629-30 at Casale Monferrato during the war for Mantua. It has been displayed in the Paris museum since 1810. Numerous copies of it are familiar, by pupils in Leonardo's circle and also by painters rather far from his school (even Flemish artists). The composition was recalled by the generation that followed Leonardo: we have only to think of the many *Madonnas* of Raphael and of the *Holy Family* (or *Doni Tondo*) of Michelangelo, which retain the figurative scheme of this *Saint Anne*, a further proof of the immediate interest and attention that each work of Leonardo's aroused as it appeared.

73. *Study for the head of St Anne*
Windsor, Royal Library

74. *Virgin and Child with St Anne, detail*
Paris, Louvre

Saint John the Baptist

75 From dark shadows this disturbing figure seems to advance painfully; the reed cross held to his chest and the animal skin which partially covers his body tell us that he is Saint John the Baptist, the Paraclete. The forefinger of his right hand is upraised, pointing to heaven, and this gesture is another element in the saint's iconography. He has come to preach penitence, to "prepare the way" for the coming of the Messiah. The face is a sharp oval, almost faun-like, framed by a cascade of curls underlined by glints of light; on the face there is an enigmatic, allusive smile, certainly unusual in the portrayal of the ascetic prophet who lived in the desert and nourished himself with locusts and wild honey. Mystery is the key word in describing this picture, surely one of Leonardo's last, to judge by its style and its expressive scope. The sources do not refer to it as a Baptist. Vasari speaks of an "angel" in the Medici collections, which he attributes to Leonardo, and the description coincides amazingly with the appearance of this Saint John. After a stay of about a hundred years in England, the panel has always been part of the collection of the rulers of France, so it cannot be the work described by Vasari. It may have been redone or transformed by the master himself or by pupils. Scholars have thus suggested that Leonardo may originally have conceived and begun an Annunciation angel, then developed it into this extraordinary figure, which undoubtedly arouses a feeling of uneasiness in the spectator rather than unconditioned admiration. And yet, in it we can discern the same spirit of problematical irony present in *La Gioconda*, expressed here, however, without the mediation of a landscape which can absorb it into a vaster system of relationships between man and nature. Therefore the *Saint John* seems more unpleasant and ambiguous to the eyes of those who observe it. In any event, the work belongs to Leonardo's production beyond a shadow of a doubt. And, as far as conception is concerned, it is the most modern of the master's works because in this figure he synthesizes all his conceptual investigation of the expression of feelings and human nature, and gives us an image charged with symbolism and allusions, purposely remaining on the boundary-line between mystery and reality. The fascination that contemporaries felt in this work is proved by the numerous copies and versions which are still preserved. Scholars place the painting in the last years of Leonardo's Roman period or the beginning of his French period (1514-1516).

75. St John the Baptist
69 x 57 cm
Paris, Louvre

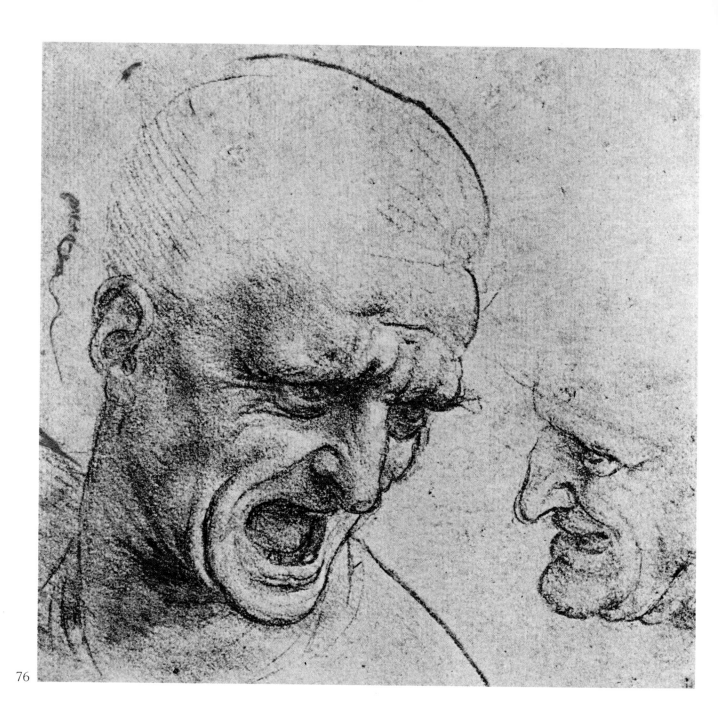

76

Violence and old age

Parallel to his production of paintings, Leonardo made a copious series of drawings, which fill the pages of his notebooks. Most of them — as we have indicated — illustrate all sorts of machinery, to be used in many branches of human activity, along with studies of a scientific nature, such as those connected with his research in mathematics, music, anatomy and botany. But there are also drawings that cannot be placed in a specific category; they are rather images that reflect Leonardo's intellectual investigations and, better than any other document,

they serve to portray his personality. In these documents we discover the artist's mental quirks, his special meditations which found, with him, a literary as well as a figurative form. There are, for example, his so-called "prophecies", which solemnly adumbrate objects, animals and everyday actions. Similarly, there are drawings of allegories or representations of human figures like the *seated old man*, 80 which lead us, with immediacy, to Leonardo's meditations on old age, and give us concretely a notion of what the artist was mentally developing,

76. *Drawing of heads, probably a study for the Battle of Anghiari*
Budapest, National Museum

77. *Copy from Leonardo*
Battle of Anghiari
Florence, Uffizi

realizing in practice the principle that — in his view — made painting coincide with philosophy, with the concept of the world in its physical and spiritual aspects. Towards the end of his life thoughts and figurative depictions of an apocalyptical character seem to predominate. This tendency of Leonardo's can be interpreted in various ways. Perhaps these are the normal reflections of a man well along in years, pondering death, but extending his thoughts to the broader theme of the end of the world and of mankind. Or perhaps he recalled, like an obsessive burden, his disappointment at works left unfinished, or lost through his constant search for new artistic techniques. An exemplary, significant instance among the works of Leonardo that were not completed is the *Battle of Anghiari*. It is significant, naturally, not only because of its fate, but also because it allowed the artist to deal with the theme of violence and human cruelty for the first time from the figurative point of view. Like the parallel *Battle of Càscina* assigned to Michelangelo, this work was commissioned by the Gonfaloniere of the Florentine Republic, Pier Soderini, in August 1504, to decorate one of the walls of what was then the Grand Council Chamber in the Palazzo della Signoria. Many of Leonardo's drawings are of clashes among mounted warriors and furious fighting among armed men. No doubt he conceived slowly his idea for the depiction of the battle in the fresco, whose central theme was the struggle for possession of the banner. Scrupulously recorded by documents, the painting was applied to the wall in 1505. But the technique with which it was executed required heat in order to dry it out. Fires were lighted in the hall, but the excessive size of the chamber did not allow a homogeneous effect, and as a result a part of the painted surface melted.

We can form an idea of the central part of the cartoon from the various copies that have been preserved. Among them there is one from a drawing of Rubens. It is a formidable conflict — fighting for the war-banner — among four horsemen and three foot-soldiers. For the first time in Leonardo, the expressions have been distorted to the limit of the hu-

79

78, 79. Drawings of cataclysms
Windsor, Royal Library

80. Drawing of a seated old man
Windsor, Royal Library

81. Map of Arezzo and the Valdichiana
Windsor, Royal Library

82. Study of trees
Windsor, Royal Library

man features' possibilities; rolling eyes, mouths opened wide in shouts meant to frighten the enemy or incite the shouter himself. The eyes of the horses also are charged with fury, and the hoofs are interwoven as the animals participate in the struggle, as if a sudden madness swept all away in its power, uniting man and beast in its irrational violence.

It seems almost impossible that the artist of *La Gioconda*, with its refined sense of measure expressed also in the subtle hint of irony, could have conceived such a terrifying scene. But we know that all of Leonardo's concepts move from a wider base, which is organized in a universal system. In it there is also room, then, for the category of violence and death. We refer to another work, whose poor state of preservation may have contributed to its loss: the *Leda*, which we know only through some preparatory drawings and derivative paintings of followers. It must be added to the number of Leonardo's works of art we no longer posses and — though it is not connected with the theme we are discussing — we mention it in the list of absences from the master's catalogue.

We know that thoughts of death and meditations on catastrophes accompanied the artist in his late activity also from the drawings of cosmic disasters on pages 12378 and 12383 of the Leonardo collection in Windsor. In the first, a whirlwind of exceptional proportions seems to strike, at the same moment, an inhabited city and the rocky mountain that dominates it, as well as the sky itself. All are overwhelmed together, creating a kind of immense explosion. In the second drawing, after every trace of human habitation has disappeared, the sea and sky are racked by a tempest of prodigious force, which no element can resist. A kind of Last Judgment, the world's last day, with only the forces of nature,

75

80

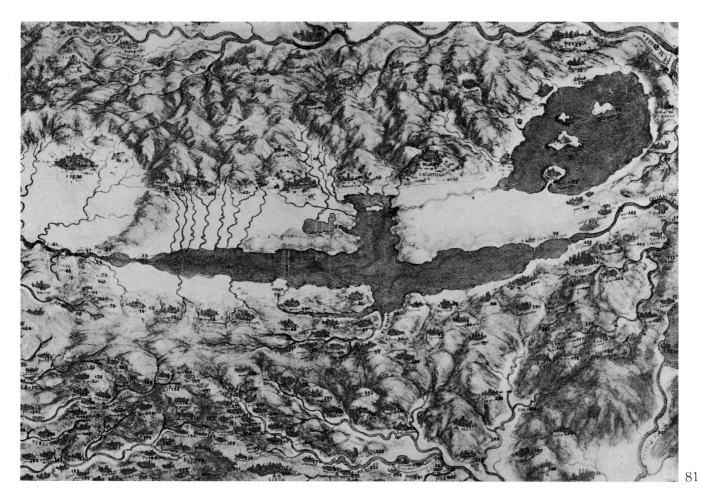

81

82

which manage to find an autonomous principle and a harmony even in this extreme destruction.

In coherence with the principle that the figurative image has the function of philosophical exposition, Leonardo then entrusted to the image the task of expressing his own concept of cosmic destruction: an equality of elements that fatally coincides with absolute harmony. It therefore begins and concludes the story of creation. Leonardo's system could not have a more logical conclusion. Then the eternal sleep could also enshroud the man whose sage's eyes and intellect, as he has left them for us in his *Self-portrait* — at once serene and severe — better than anyone else had investigated the mysteries of the world and its laws, man and his feelings; and in the most sublime way had known how to express and communicate them to others through his art.

83. Drawing with self-portrait
Turin, National Library

Basic Bibliography

G. VASARI, *Le vite. . .*, Firenze, 1568

G. UZIELLI, *Ricerche intorno a Leonardo da Vinci*, Firenze, 1872

E. MÜNTZ, *Léonard de Vinci*, Paris, 1899

O. SIRÉN, *Leonardo da Vinci*, Stockholm, 1911

L. BELTRAMI, *Documenti e memorie riguardanti la vita. . . di Leonardo*, Milano, 1919

A. ROSENBERG, *Leonardo da Vinci*, Leipzig, 1919

A. VENTURI, *Leonardo da Vinci pittore*, Bologna, 1920

W. VON BODE, *Studien über Leonardo*, Berlin, 1921

E. HILDEBRANDT, *Leonardo da Vinci*, Berlin, 1928

W. SUIDA, *Leonardo und sein Kreis*, München, 1929

H. BODMER, *Leonardo*, Stuttgart, 1931

K. CLARK, *Leonardo da Vinci*, Cambridge, 1939

S. BOTTARI, *Leonardo*, Bergamo, 1942

A. VALENTIN, *Léonard de Vinci*, Paris, 1950

Leonardo. Saggi e ricerche, Roma, 1952

G. CASTELFRANCO, *Leonardo da Vinci*, Milano, 1952

L. H. HEYDENREICH, *Leonardo da Vinci*, Basel, 1954

C. BARONI, *Tutta la pittura di Leonardo*, Milano, 1962

A. OTTINO DELLA CHIESA, *L'opera completa di Leonardo pittore*, Milano, 1967

La scheda d'arte. Leonardo. Tutta la pittura, Firenze, 1988

Index of Illustrations